Meet the dinosaurs

Before you start reading *Towering Brachiosaurus*, let's meet its main characters. Who are they? What do they look like? And where did they live?

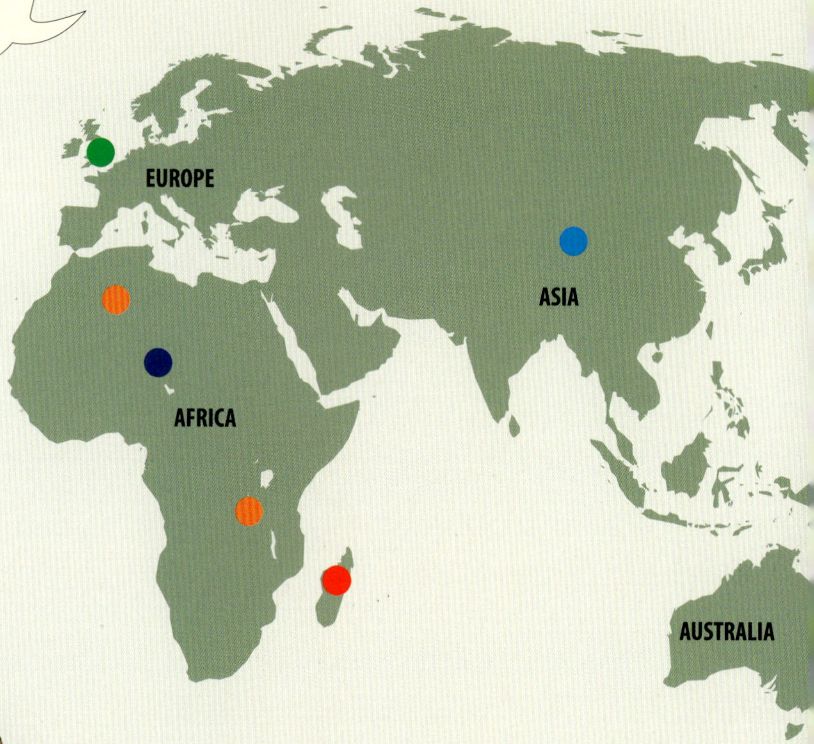

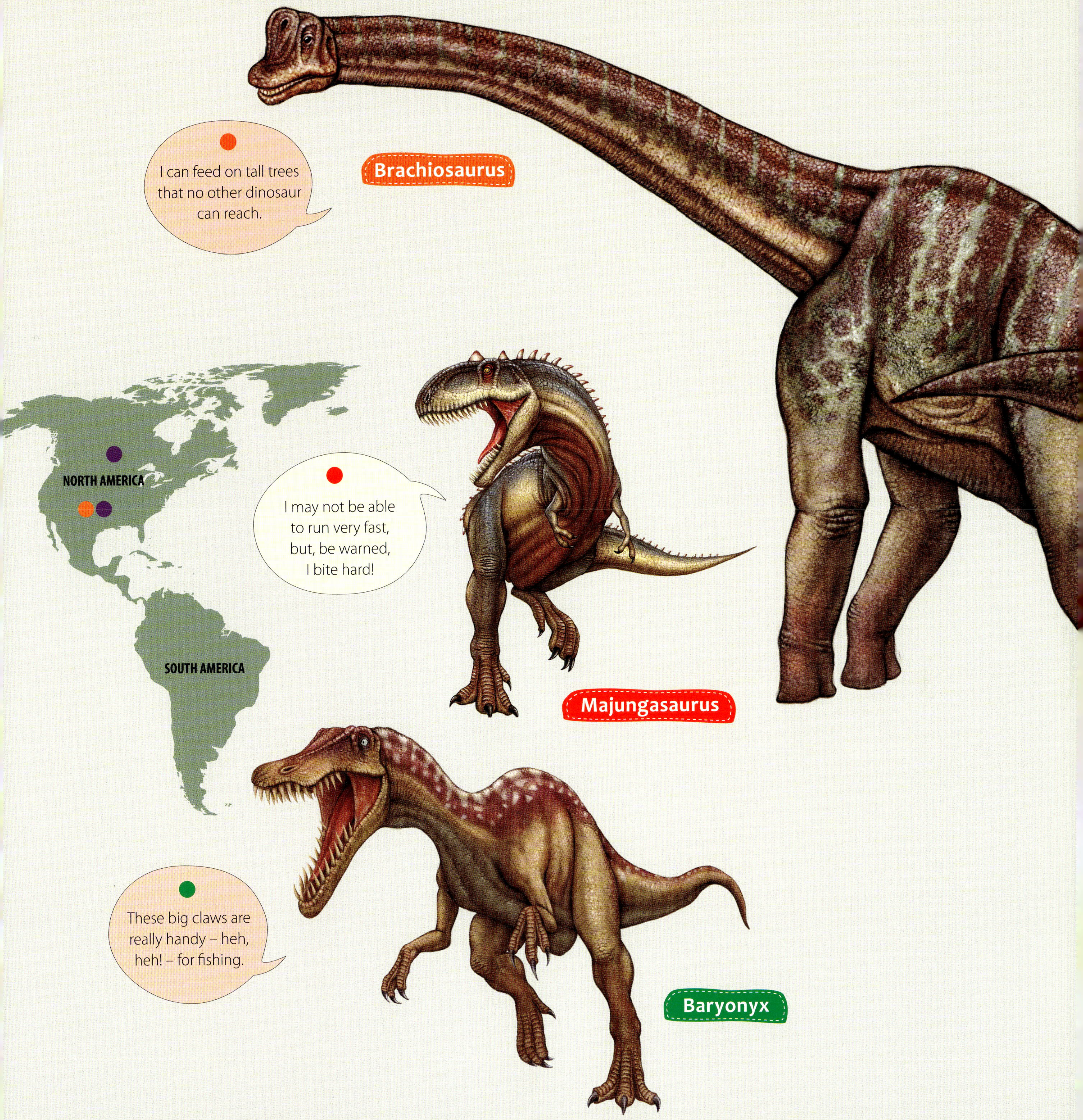
I can feed on tall trees that no other dinosaur can reach.
Brachiosaurus
NORTH AMERICA
SOUTH AMERICA
I may not be able to run very fast, but, be warned, I bite hard!
Majungasaurus
These big claws are really handy – heh, heh! – for fishing.
Baryonyx

Original Korean text and illustrations by Dreaming Tortoise

This English edition published by big & SMALL in 2016
by arrangement with Aram Publishing
English text edited by Scott Forbes

Distributed in the United States and Canada by
Lerner Publishing Group, Inc.
241 First Avenue North
Minneapolis, MN 55401 U.S.A.
www.lernerbooks.com

Photo credits:
Page 28, top: © Kabacch; middle: © Ballista
Page 29, middle: © D. Gordon E. Robertson;
bottom: © Ripton Scott

ISBN: 978-1-925248-77-7
Printed in Korea

To learn about dinosaur fossils, see page 28.
For information on the main groups of dinosaurs, see the Dinosaur Family Tree on page 30.

Towering **Brachiosaurus**

big & SMALL

Afrovenator

SAY IT:
AFF-roh-ven-ay-tor

Two Afrovenators were chasing a Vulcanodon. The Vulcanodon was running short of breath. It couldn't keep going.

The Afrovenators closed in on either side. With a roar, they pounced on the Vulcanodon and dragged it to the ground to eat.

VULCANODON

GROUP: Sauropods
DIET: Plants
WHEN IT LIVED: Early Jurassic
WHERE IT LIVED: Africa
LENGTH: 20–23 feet (6–7 meters)
HEIGHT: 8 feet (2.5 meters)
WEIGHT: 5.5–7.7 tons (5–7 tonnes)

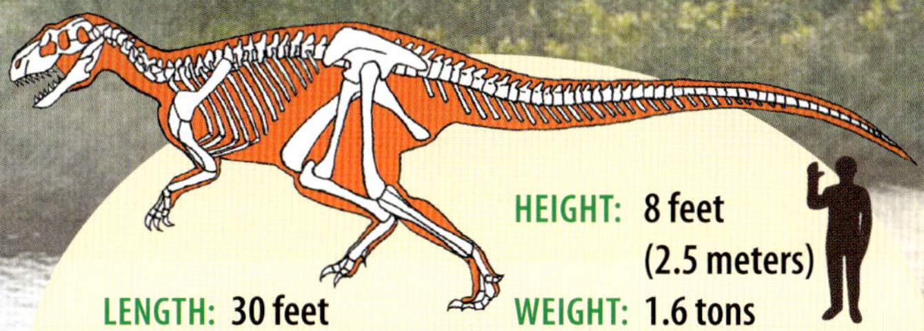

LENGTH: 30 feet (9 meters)
HEIGHT: 8 feet (2.5 meters)
WEIGHT: 1.6 tons (1.5 tonnes)

WHEN IT LIVED: TRIASSIC JURASSIC CRETACEOUS

GROUP: Theropods
DIET: Meat

WHERE IT LIVED: Africa

Afrovenator means "African hunter." This dinosaur was the fiercest hunter, or predator, in Africa. No other dinosaur could challenge it.

Afrovenator wasn't especially fast. But it had powerful jaws, long sharp teeth, and strong front claws. It could tackle almost any prey.

Afrovenator may have been related to a similar-sized European meat-eater called Megalosaurus.

Tuojiangosaurus

SAY IT:
Too-oh-jang-oh-SAW-rus

Two Tuojiangosaurus plodded steadily through the forest. It was a hot day, and they were on their way to the river to have a long, cool drink of water.

Tuojiangosaurus means "lizard from the Tuo River." This river in China is where the first fossils of this dinosaur were found.

Tuojiangosaurus was about the size of a car. It had pointed plates all along its back and long, sharp spikes on its tail.

As the Tuojiangosaurus neared the river, they came face to face with a fierce hunter, Yangchuanosaurus. It circled them and looked like it was ready to attack.

Tuojiangosaurus had a small head and a small brain and was probably not the smartest of dinosaurs. But it knew how to defend itself.

The Tuojiangosaurus stood side by side and swung their spiky tails at their attacker. The Yangchuanosaurus could see that those spikes might hurt it badly. So it simply roared at the Tuojiangosaurus and went on its way.

Chasmosaurus

SAY IT:
Kaz-mo-SAW-rus

A family of Chasmosaurus were being attacked by an Albertosaurus. The baby Chasmosaurus hid between its father and mother. The adults prepared to defend themselves. If necessary, they were ready to charge the Albertosaurus and stab it with their sharp horns.

Chasmosaurus had three large horns and a huge neck frill that stood up straight at the back of its head. When viewed from the front, the frill made its head look enormous. That put some hunters off attacking Chasmosaurus.

ALBERTOSAURUS

GROUP: Theropods
DIET: Meat
WHEN IT LIVED: Late Cretaceous
WHERE IT LIVED: North America (Canada, USA)
LENGTH: 30 feet (9 meters)
HEIGHT: 13 feet (4 meters)
WEIGHT: 1.6 tons (1.5 tonnes)

LENGTH: 16.5 feet (5 meters) HEIGHT: 8 feet (2.5 meters) WEIGHT: 1.4 tons (1.3 tonnes)

WHEN IT LIVED: TRIASSIC JURASSIC CRETACEOUS

GROUP: Ceratopsians

DIET: Plants

WHERE IT LIVED:
North America
(Canada, USA)

Brachiosaurus

SAY IT:
Brak-ee-oh-SAW-rus

A group of Brachiosaurus were feeding in the forest. They stretched their long necks upward to reach the highest branches. All at once, they realized a group of Ceratosaurus were circling them, trying to seize one of their young.

Brachiosaurus's legs were up to 40 feet (12 meters) tall. That meant it could reach high up into the trees to feed on leaves other plant-eating dinosaurs couldn't reach.

Just one adult Brachiosaurus weighed as much as 10 of today's African elephants. To maintain its body weight it had to eat 2.2 tons (2 tonnes) of plants every day.

CERATOSAURUS

GROUP: Theropods
DIET: Meat
WHEN IT LIVED: Late Jurassic
WHERE IT LIVED: Africa (Tanzania)
LENGTH: 20–33 feet (6–10 meters)
HEIGHT: 8 feet (2.5 meters)
WEIGHT: 1.1 tons (1 tonne)

The young Brachiosaurus ran between the adults to hide. Then the adult Brachiosaurus swung their long, heavy tails and scared the Ceratosaurus away.

Majungasaurus

SAY IT:
Mah-yoong-ah-SAW-rus

Two Majungasaurus leaped out from behind some bushes and dashed toward a group of Rapetosaurus. The Rapetosaurus rushed away in all directions, but together the two Majungasaurus chased after one of them and caught it.

RAPETOSAURUS

GROUP: Sauropods
DIET: Plants
WHEN IT LIVED: Late Cretaceous
WHERE IT LIVED: Africa (Madagascar)
LENGTH: 50 feet (15 meters)
HEIGHT: 16.5 feet (5 meters)
WEIGHT: 13.2 tons (12 tonnes)

For a big, meat-eating dinosaur, Majungasaurus had a fairly small head. It also had quite short legs and could not run very fast. But its neck and jaw muscles were powerful, so it could bite hard. It often hunted long-necked, plant-eating dinosaurs like Rapetosaurus.

The Majungasaurus dragged the Rapetosaurus down to the lakeshore to eat it. But then the larger Majungasaurus tried to chase the other one away. It growled and roared. Clearly it didn't want to share the food!

The two Majungasaurus fought furiously, scratching and snapping, till the smaller one backed off and crept away, still growling.

Majungasaurus had a very wide head and jaws, and a short horn on its head. If it was very hungry, Majungasaurus sometimes ate other Majungasaurus.

HEIGHT: 6.6 feet (2 meters)

LENGTH: 23 feet (7 meters)

WEIGHT: 1.6 tons (1.5 tonnes)

WHEN IT LIVED: TRIASSIC JURASSIC CRETACEOUS

GROUP: Theropods

DIET: Meat

WHERE IT LIVED: Africa (Madagasar)

Baryonyx

SAY IT:
Bah-ree-ON-icks

Two Baryonyx were hunting for fish. They peered into the water, waiting patiently. A fish swam silently into view. One Baryonyx thrust its arm into the water, spearing the fish on a long claw. It lifted the fish to its jaws, then swallowed it in one gulp.

Baryonyx means "strong claw." The claw on its first finger was longer than the others — about 12 inches (30 centimeters) long. Baryonyx used this claw like a harpoon, to spear prey, especially fish.

It wasn't just fish that Baryonyx ate, however. When other dinosaurs came down to the water to drink, Baryonyx would hide in bushes or trees. Then it would pounce on prey, such as Iguanodon.

Baryonyx did not have a powerful bite. But it could still catch an Iguanodon by grasping it in its long, sharp claws.

Dinosaur Fossils

Fossils are the remains of dinosaurs. They can be hard parts of dinosaurs, such as bones and teeth, that have slowly turned to stone. Or they may be impressions of bones, teeth, or skin preserved in rocks.

▲ Model of Afrovenator skeleton

Afrovenator

Afrovenator was an African relative of Allosaurus, a fearsome North American predator, and looked quite similar. The first Afrovenator fossil was found in the Sahara Desert, in Niger, in 1994, by dinosaur hunter Paul Sereno. It was an almost complete skeleton, so it provided a lot of information about this dinosaur.

Tuojiangosaurus

Tuojiangosaurus was the first dinosaur with back plates to be found in Asia. It was discovered in the mid-1970s in Sichuan Province, China, and studied and named by a famous Chinese dinosaur hunter, Dong Zhiming. A magnificent Tuojiangosaurus skeleton is on display in the Chongqing Museum in Sichuan, China.

▲ Tuojiangosaurus tailbone

▲ Model of Chasmosaurus skeleton

Chasmosaurus

Canadian dinosaur hunter Lawrence Lambe found the first fossil of Chasmosaurus in Alberta, Canada, in 1898. At first he thought it was a fossil of a dinosaur called Monoclonious, which was the only horned dinosaur to have been discovered at that point. But in 1913 dinosaur hunter Charles Hazelius Sternberg and his sons found similar fossils in the same area, including several skulls. This made it clear that this was a completely new kind of dinosaur.

Brachiosaurus

Brachiosaurus fossils were first found in 1900 in Colorado, USA, by Elmer S. Riggs. For a long time, Brachiosaurus was thought to be part of a family of dinosaurs called the brontosaurs. But when a complete skeleton of Brachiosaurus was found in Tanzania, Africa, in 1914, scientists realized it was a different kind of dinosaur, and they named it Brachiosaurus.

▲ Model of Brachiosaurus skeleton

Majungasaurus

Scientists first found Majungasaurus fossils in the late 1800s, on the large island of Madagascar, off the southeast coast of Africa. At first they thought the fossils belonged to Megalosaurus. But in 1955 scientists decided the fossils were from a similar but different kind of dinosaur. They named it Majungasaurus after the Majunga Desert, where the fossils were found.

▲ Model of Majungasaurus skeleton

Baryonyx

It was an amateur fossil hunter called William Walker who found the first Baryonyx fossil, in England in 1983. It was a huge hand claw, about 12 inches (30 centimeters) long. Scientists then explored the place where Walker had found the claw and discovered an entire skeleton. Three years later, the dinosaur was given its name.

▲ Model of Baryonyx skeleton

THE DINOSAUR FAMILY TREE

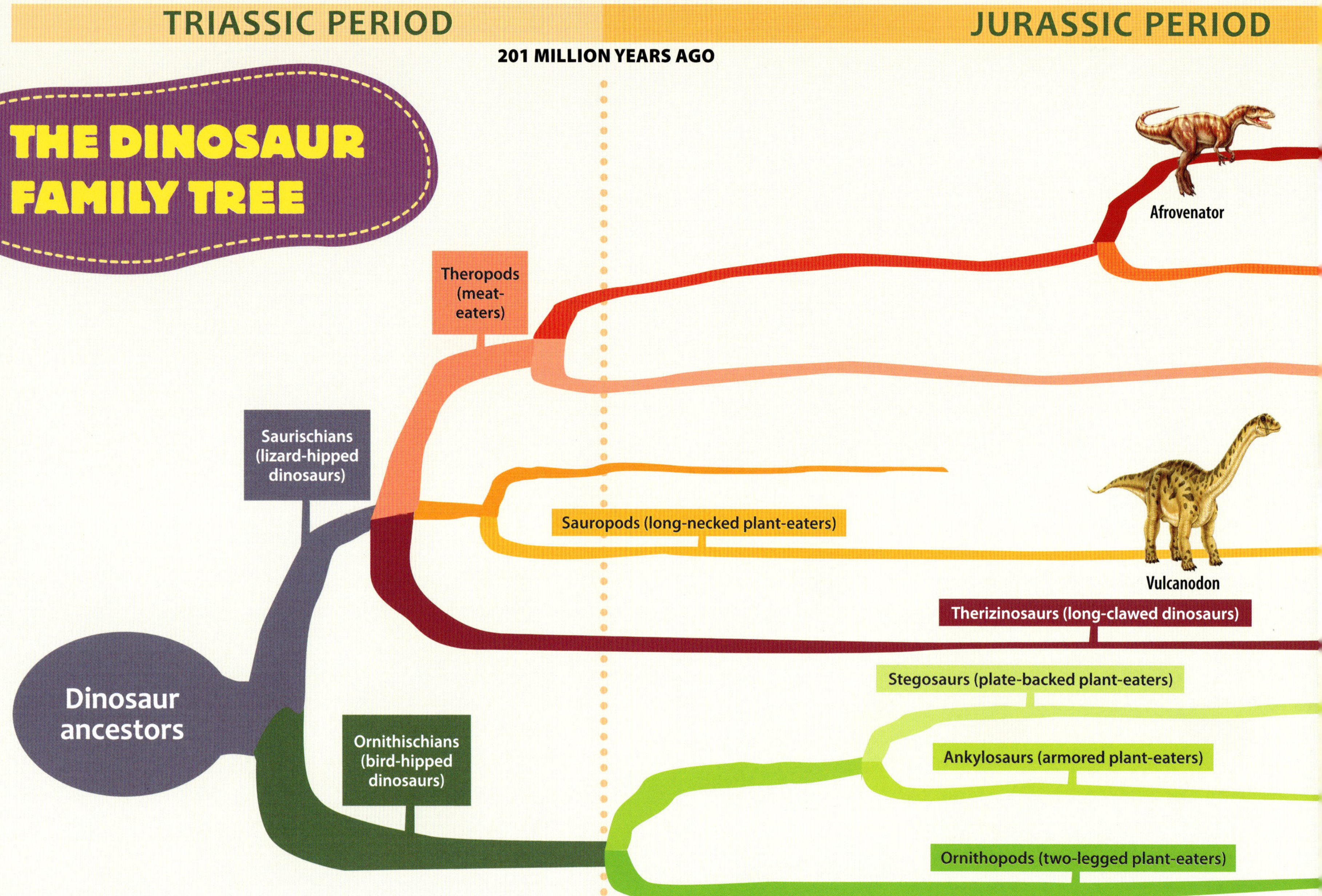

Dinosaurs lived on Earth from about 245 million years ago until about 66 million years ago — long before the first humans. After the first dinosaurs appeared, they spread to all the continents and many different kinds of dinosaurs emerged. This chart shows the main groups of dinosaurs.

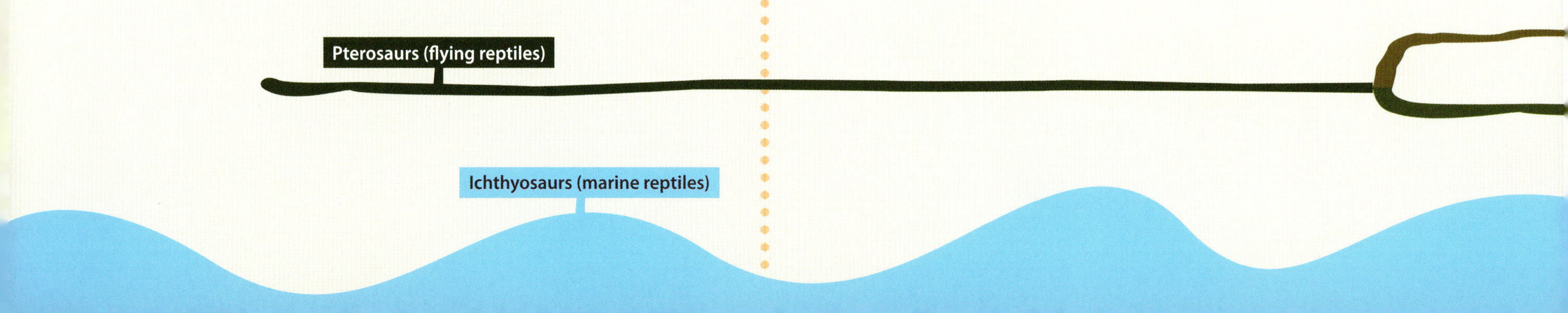

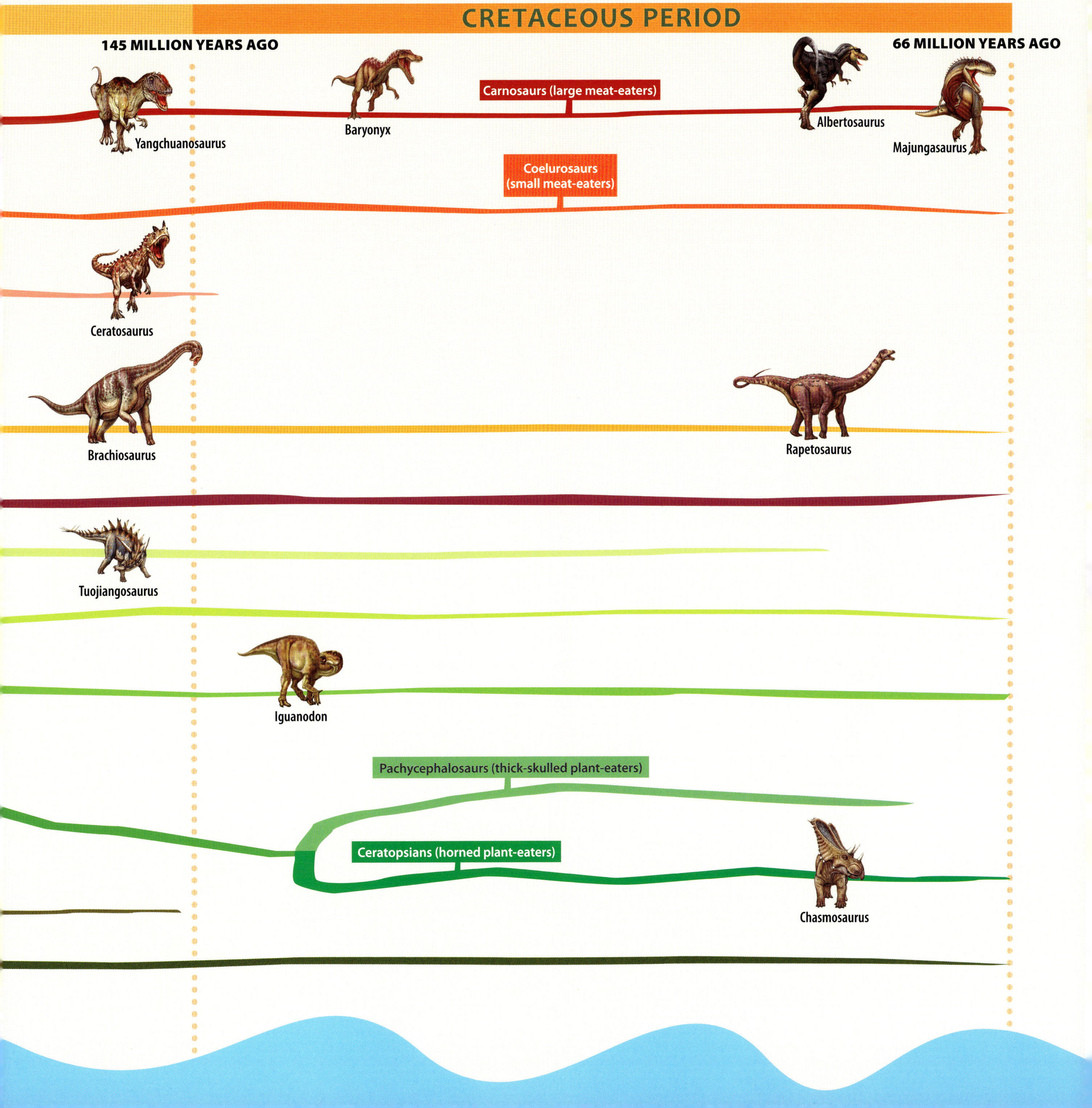

CRETACEOUS PERIOD
145 MILLION YEARS AGO
66 MILLION YEARS AGO
Carnosaurs (large meat-eaters)
Yangchuanosaurus
Baryonyx
Albertosaurus
Majungasaurus
Coelurosaurs (small meat-eaters)
Ceratosaurus
Brachiosaurus
Rapetosaurus
Tuojiangosaurus
Iguanodon
Pachycephalosaurs (thick-skulled plant-eaters)
Ceratopsians (horned plant-eaters)
Chasmosaurus